WHY DO PARAKEETS DO THAT?

Real Answers to the Curious Things Parakeets Do

By Nikki Moustaki
Illustrations by Buck Jones

IRVINE, CALIFORNIA

Ruth Strother, Project Manager
Nick Clemente, Special Consultant
Michelle Martinez, Editor; Karla Austin, Associate Editor
Michael Vincent Capozzi, Designer

The birds in this book are referred to as *he* and *she* in alternating chapters.

Library of Congress Cataloging-in-Publication Data

Moustaki, Nikki, 1970-
Why do parakeets do that? : real answers to the curious things parakeets do / by Nikki Moustaki ; illustrations by Buck Jones.
p. cm.
ISBN 1-889540-97-8 (pbk. : alk. paper)
1. Parrots--Miscellanea. I. Title.

SF473.P3 M68 2003
636.6'864--dc21
2002014079

BowTie™ Press
A DIVISION OF FANCY PUBLICATIONS
3 Burroughs
Irvine, California 92618
949-855-8822

Printed and Bound in Singapore
10 9 8 7 6 5 4 3 2 1

For all of my wonderful editors at
Fancy Publications.

—N.M.

For my good friends the Burger Brothers.

—B.J.

Contents

Why Do Parakeets Sometimes Go by the Name of Budgie?

The term *parakeet* is a generic name for all of the parrotlike birds having long, tapering tails rather than blunt, square tails. The term *budgie* is actually more specific, referring directly to our beloved *Melopsittacus undulates*. In the United States, the budgie is commonly known as the American parakeet, which is kind of silly, considering that this bird originated in Australia. The word *budgie* comes from the aboriginal Australian word for this bird, *betchegara*, meaning "good to eat." But please, don't eat your parakeets. There isn't a good recipe for them yet!

There are other names for the parakeet as well, but you will

most commonly see this bird called budgie or parakeet. These two names basically can be used interchangeably. For the purposes of this book, we'll refer to *Melopsittacus undulates* primarily as "parakeet". But, if the pet shop sells you a budgie, you've still got the right book in your hands.

Why Do Parakeets Come Supersized?

That "giant" parakeet you see at the pet shop isn't a science experiment. It's an English budgie, the stout cousin to the slender American parakeet. Like all parakeets, this bird was cultivated from the wild parakeet, but its breeders concentrated on the bird's size and shape. The English budgie was developed primarily for exhibition, though it makes a great companion too. There's little difference in temperament between the English budgie and the parakeet, though the English budgie is said to be mellower. The only drawback to the English budgie is that it has about half the life expectancy as that of the parakeet.

HI. HOW YOU DOING?

How a Parakeet's Feathers Work as Camouflage

The American parakeet's scientific name is *Melopsittacus undulates*, meaning "song bird with wavy lines." These lines are great camouflage for the parakeet as it moves about in the tall grasses of Australia. The parakeet's lines make it difficult for predators to pick an individual out of the flock. Imagine hundreds of birds and tens of thousands of wavy lines all moving in frenzied patterns across the sky—chaos!

Why Do Parakeets Bond with Humans?

Single parakeets bond with their human owners largely because they have no other choice. They are programmed to think going solo is not only lonely but dangerous. (Besides, aren't we a cool species, worthy of parakeet love?) But what's a parakeet to do when he's a lone bird in a human household? Fortunately, the parakeet is an adaptable animal. Instead of searching endlessly for other parakeets, the companion parakeet comes to regard his human companions as part of his flock. Not only do human flock members provide security and company, but they provide food and water as well.

For the most part, a companion parakeet does whatever it

takes to become a part of the flock, even if he's the only flock member with feathers. He may learn to whistle or mimic the language of the flock, he may call tirelessly for his human companions, and he may even find a human "mate" in the home and court him or her with as much amour as he would another parakeet. These behaviors indicate a happy parakeet who's getting along well in his home, even if the other members of his flock are quite naked of feathers and aren't even green.

Why Do Parakeets Come in So Many Colors and Patterns?

Parakeets don't come in a variety of colors just to match your drapes and sofa, nor are they found in the wild in the vast array of colors that occur in captive bred parakeets. In the wild, where it's world is primarily green and striped with tall grasses (*it's* drapes are green!), the parakeet's primary color is green. Green is a good color for a parakeet, because a bird has to blend in with her surroundings or she'll end up being an appetizer for a predator in the outback.

The pretty colors that companion parakeets are found in today are mutations and are a naturally occurring event, like albinism. A blue, yellow, or white parakeet stands out in the

MoMMM!!!! WHERE'S THE PARAKEET?

wild, making her an easy mark for hawks and other predators. This leaves little opportunity for her to pass along her genes to her babies. So, the flock stays green.

Once people began breeding parakeets, they occasionally found a baby of another color in the nest box. This was a boon for breeders, who could then breed that baby hoping that the color would repeat itself. Using the principles of genetics, breeders are able to reproduce a color mutation successfully. This is how we came to have all the beautifully colored parakeets that we have today.

Is Your Parakeet a Boy or a Girl?

Determining the gender of your parakeet is pretty easy after he or she has reached maturity, which is at about six to eight months, perhaps sooner. The fleshy spot, called the cere, just above the beak that contains the nostrils becomes blue in adult males and pink or brown in adult females. In baby parakeets, however, the cere is whitish pinkish bluish—an indefinite color indicating that the parakeet is still quite young.

Why Do Parakeets Whistle, Talk, and Constantly Chatter?

The parakeet is one of the most proficient talkers in the parrot world. Some birds have been recorded speaking hundreds of words and phrases. Parakeets are also great at whistling and can learn to whistle many songs. Male parakeets are reputed to talk with more frequency and clarity than females but there are exceptions.

Most people enjoy the constant *chit chit chit chitty chit* of their parakeets and come to love the whistling, cheeping, singing, peeping, talking, and other sounds that their birds make. But even those people who enjoy the noise sometimes wonder why their birds have to keep it up all day long!

PET
STORE

Parakeets talk because they like us. They are paying attention to our world and mimicking it. Sharing a common language is part of the social structure of birds, so it's natural that parakeets would want to contribute their two cents worth to the vocalizations in the household.

If you want a parakeet who's going to be vocal, start thinking about this as early as when you select your bird. Watch a group of parakeets and choose the one who's making the most racket—that's a bird who likes to vocalize and may learn to talk well.

Most birds vocalize at dawn and at dusk. This is normal and can't really be stopped. There are periods of quiet during the day when a parakeet is eating, napping, or playing on his own, but for the most part, parakeets vocalize. Being a small social bird, the parakeet is programmed to assert his presence,

CHATTER · CHATTER · CHATTER ·
CHATTER · CHATTER · CHATTER ·
CHATTER · CHATTER · CHATTER ·
CHATTER · CHATTER · CHATTER ·
CHATTER · CHATTER....

keep up with his mate, and let the others in his flock know when he's okay, distressed, and so on. If there are a lot of birds to "talk" to, there's going to be a lot of vocalizing.

Teaching a bird anything is all about repetition. Once you decide what you want your parakeet to learn to say, simply repeat it over and over as clearly as possible. It's important to sound excited and enthusiastic when you say the word or phrase because birds are attracted to energy, and the more energy you put into what you're trying to teach him, the faster he will learn. This is why birds learn "no!" "be quiet!" and curse words *way* too easily!

Why Do Parakeets Become Addicted to Seeds?

Wild parakeets feed primarily on both young and mature seeds. They are opportunistic and will eat as much of whatever is growing at the time. The house parakeet who is fed primarily seeds will gorge on seeds because she is programmed to do so. When seeds are around, she will prefer them over anything else.

Unfortunately, dry seeds don't have the nutritional value that young seeds and sprouts do, which means that the seed-addicted parakeet is getting a lot of calories without the same amount of nutrition. Ultimately, this can lead to a fat parakeet with liver problems, fatty tumors, and gout. Seeds aren't bad

for your parakeet when fed in moderation as a part of the total diet, which should include veggies; fruit; specially cooked birdie foods; pellets; and safe, healthy table foods.

Food Tips for Your Parakeet

• The best veggies and fruits to feed your parakeet are dark green or dark orange in color.

• Make sure you wash all produce well before offering it to your bird.

• Never feed your parakeet alcohol, chocolate, or caffeine, all of which can be deadly.

• Part of the avocado pit is toxic to birds, so avoid avocado too.

• Raw rhubarb isn't recommended.

• Raw onions and tomatoes aren't toxic, your parakeet just won't like them.

• Seeds in any fruit or veggies, except melons and squashes, can be toxic, so take them out before feeding these items to your bird.

• Parakeets do not need the supplement grit, and can even die if they gorge on it.

• Parakeets will appreciate a cuttlebone and mineral block in the cage.

• If you offer your bird chicken eggs, which are high in nutrition, boil them for at least thirty minutes to avoid any avian diseases that may have come with the egg.

Why Do Parakeets Like to Look in the Mirror?

They're vain, oh so vain. Well, that's not really the reason, though it seems as likely a reason as any other. Parakeets are social animals who prefer parakeet companions over human companions—there are exceptions, but that's generally the rule. A single parakeet with access to a mirror may become enamored with his own reflection and try to woo the "other bird." Your parakeet is not a dope. He's just lonely for his own kind. Parakeets may also fall in love with a common plastic toy that looks like a parakeet. Will the real bird please stand up? If your parakeet becomes absolutely obsessed with the mirror or look-alike toy and doesn't respond to you the way

he used to, remove the toy and give him more attention. Or consider getting your bird a live parakeet friend.

Why Do Parakeets Wear Jewelry?

You might have wondered about the band on your parakeet's leg. No, it's not a new parakeet jewelry trend. This band was put on by the breeder when your parakeet was just a little pink baby. Baby parakeets have the same barring on their heads as they have on their wings. As they grow older, these head stripes disappear and are replaced by a solid color. Once the bars are gone, however, it's hard to tell a three-year-old bird from an eight-year-old bird—unless there's a leg band.

Each leg band is engraved with the breeder's initials, state abbreviation, and the month and year in which the parakeet was hatched. This is the only real way you can be certain of your parakeet's age.

SO, HOW OLD ARE YOU?
LET ME CHECK.

Why Do Parakeets Like to Take Baths?

Parakeets know instinctively that keeping clean is important to flight, a parakeet's primary defense mechanism. Dirty birds have a more difficult time flying than birds with clean feathers. Birds are excellent at energy conservation, and dirt can cause a bird to expend more energy than needed. The house parakeet has the same instinctive programming as the wild parakeet, so a clean, temperate dish of water is going to look like the perfect opportunity to bathe. Bathing also helps keep the skin from becoming dry and itchy, and it's a nice way to cool down on a hot day.

HERS

Why Do Parakeets Sleep on One Foot?

Parakeets aren't showing off their bountiful balancing ability when they're sleeping on one foot. A parakeet's legs are not covered with feathers, making them vulnerable to heat loss, especially during sleep, when the body temperature drops. The parakeet tucks one leg into her stomach feathers for warmth.

A parakeet sleeping while standing on both feet might be cause for concern since that may be a symptom of illness (or perhaps it's just too cold in the room). If you notice that your parakeet is sleeping while standing on two feet, feathers puffed, eyes droopy, or is displaying any other symptoms of illness, take her to your avian veterinarian right away.

Bbbrrrrrr...
1:51 AM

Why Do Parakeets Like to Do Aerobics?

If most healthy parakeets had to take the President's physical fitness test, they would pass with flying (literally) colors. Parakeets love to flap their wings, clamber around the cage, fly (if they're unclipped), and perform other feats of aerobic prowess, such as hanging upside down in the cage, crawling up and down their little birdie ladders and the overhead wooden toy lift. The parakeet is a bird with a high metabolism, which enables him to fly many miles a day. The house parakeet generally isn't allowed to fly, so he needs to expend his pent-up energy by means of other exercise.

Parakeets who spend their lives in small cages usually

develop health problems, including obesity and tumors. A diet high in carbohydrates and fat combined with the lack of proper exercise is the culprit. Either provide your parakeet with an aviary, or play actively with him by having him climb up a rope or a ladder, or by putting him on your finger and dropping your hand gently until he flaps his wings to right himself. Don't force him to do exercises that frighten him, but do find exercises that are more like play, and include them in your daily routine.

Why Do Parakeets Attack Their Toys?

Parakeets aren't as aggressive as some of the other commonly kept parrots, but they aren't docile little creatures either. Squabbles break out frequently among pairs or groups of parakeets, and it's not unusual for one or two parakeets in an aviary to bully others. But what about the parakeet who's all alone, with only her toys for company during the day? That parakeet has no choice but to befriend her toys, and in every good friendship there is conflict. She may sidle up to a plastic parakeet toy for some affection, and when it doesn't respond to her advances, she may choose to beat it savagely instead. Mirror toys are treated with similar hostility—the

parakeet in the mirror is behaving antagonistically, so why shouldn't it receive a savage beating? Other toys are prone to rough play as well, especially toys with bells or other toys that make noise. Parakeets love to assert themselves onto their environment, and there's no better reward for that activity than a ringing bell.

Why Do Parakeets Like to Live Together?

Parakeets are one of the many species of birds who live in flocks ranging from several birds to thousands. Flocking is one of the parakeet's natural defenses against predators. Since parakeets feed primarily on the ground where they're vulnerable, having a lot of friends around is particularly helpful. One parakeet who is feeding or preening is not likely to notice a predator lurking, but one out of hundreds of parakeets probably will, and that bird's panic will alert the others to the danger.

Parakeets also rely on their flock members for company, mutual preening, mating, raising chicks, and so on. They make great aviary birds if the aviary is large enough, and they do

I'M SO EXCITED TO HAVE YOU LIVE WITH ME!
HANDLE WITH CARE
TOYS

well in pairs. They like to live together for the same reason that many other animals like to live together—it's more fun to have company than to be alone, with only your thoughts and your mirror toy for entertainment. The parakeet is a social bird and is programmed to have a mate (or at least a pal); his instincts tell him that he's supposed to have other parakeet friends, and those instincts are more powerful than anything he can learn from living in a human home.

Why Do Parakeets Lose Their Feathers?

Feathers are sturdy structures, but they aren't indestructible. They get torn and raggedy and need to be replaced. A healthy parakeet goes though a molt once or twice a year. This is akin to a snake or lizard losing his skin, but instead of losing skin, a bird loses feathers and grows new ones.

Though there will be feathers all over the bottom of the cage and surrounding areas, there's nothing to worry about. Some people become alarmed by the sight of so many feathers, but there's nothing to be concerned about unless you see bald patches on your bird. Molting birds do not lose feathers in clumps, so there should be no visible difference in the bird's

feathering, except for the waxy sheaths, or pin feathers, growing in underneath the old feathers. These sheathes are made of keratin, the same material that composes our fingernails. Your parakeet will spend a lot of time opening these sheathes to let the new feathers emerge more easily. She might need help with the feathers on top of her head, so if you and your parakeet are great friends, gently crush the sheathes with a fingernail when your bird offers you her head for preening. These sheathes can be painful and the feathers inside of them have a blood supply, so act slowly and gently. Lightly misting your parakeet with clean, tepid water helps to soften these sheathes and makes feather growth a little less irritating. Bathing during molting time is important and encourages preening.

Your parakeet is especially sensitive during a molt and may become cranky and not want to come out of her cage. She may not even behave like her perky self. This is because growing new feathers to replace old ones takes a lot of energy, and your parakeet is simply darn tired! Also, the feathers that are growing in tend to be itchy and are sometimes painful, so your parakeet may just want to chill out and not be bothered for a while. When the molt is over in a few weeks to a few months, your bird will be back to normal.

Molting Parakeet Cake Crumble

Feed your parakeet extra protein during a molt. Hard-boiled eggs, sprouted beans, and pieces of chicken are good sources of protein. Feed dark green and orange veggies and fruits in abundance as well—carrots, kale, cantaloupe, and cooked squash are good choices. Here's a recipe that molting parakeets will appreciate. You can offer this food all year long too.

- 1 package corn muffin mix
- 1 egg (as indicated on muffin package), including shell
- ¼ cup spinach, chopped (fresh or frozen)
- ¼ cup fresh carrots, grated
- ¼ cup beans, any type, sprouted or from a can (not dry)
- ¼ cup mixed dried fruit
- ¼ cup small bird pellets, organic
- 2 teaspoons calcium powder (optional)

Mix the corn muffin mix according to the package. If the package calls for an egg, use the whole egg, including the crushed shell. If it does not call for an egg, hard-boil an egg, crush it, and add it along with the rest of the ingredients. Once the mix is blended, add the other ingredients and stir well. Bake in a greased cake pan according to the directions on the package, allowing extra time for the other ingredients to bake—it may take twice as long as indicated. When a knife comes out of the center clean, cool the cake on a wire rack. Crumble it into large chunks and freeze. Thaw a portion each day and offer it to your parakeet.

Why Do Parakeets Preen Themselves (and One Another—or You!)?

When a parakeet preens himself he runs his beak through his feathers, making sure that each one is clean and neatly "zipped up." Feathers are made of fine strands that zip together. If these strands aren't closed and clean, it is difficult for the bird to maintain his body temperature or to fly.

Preening is a normal daily behavior and is a sign of a healthy bird. Bathing prompts preening, as does molting. A parakeet has a gland at the base of his tail that secretes oil used to keep the feathers supple and waterproof. The parakeet will pick up some of this oil with his beak and run it though his feathers. The only place that a parakeet can't preen is the top of his head, a duty he may want his mate or you to perform.

Mutual preening, or allopreening, is a normal event in the daily life of a parakeet living in a pair or group. Allopreening functions both to reinforce the bond between two birds and to ensure that feathers in unreachable places get preened too. A parakeet living alone doesn't have the benefit of allopreening, and will want you to understudy as a bird and learn how to preen. A human-bonded parakeet who's comfortable with you and his environment will put his head down and offer you his neck as an invitation for preening. Scratch his head and neck lightly, ruffling the feathers rather than smoothing them down. Be gentle and preen only the head and neck unless your parakeet indicates that you may proceed further.

To a parakeet, hair is the human equivalent to feathers. You

might find that your bird likes to preen your hair, eyebrows, mustache, or beard. This is quite endearing and shows that your parakeet trusts you and considers you worth his interest.

How Your Parakeet Keeps Warm

Feathers are nature's best temperature control devises, able to keep a bird both cool *and* warm, depending on what's needed. A parakeet fluffs his feathers when he's feeling a little cold, trapping air close to his skin so that the air can be warmed and kept underneath the feathers, the same way a down jacket keeps a person warm by trapping the air beneath the jacket.

Being a little fluffy is okay when a parakeet is sleeping at night or if the weather is particularly cold, but it isn't a normal permanent state for a parakeet. When a bird feels ill or too cold, he tries to keep his body temperature high by remaining fluffed. If you notice that your parakeet is fluffy and sleepy during hours when he should be awake and perky, consult your avian veterinarian.

Parakeets also do a quick, tension-releasing fluff of the whole body that helps to get rid of trapped debris in the feathers after preening and provides a moment of stress relief—a little like birdie yoga.

Why Do Parakeets Poop So Often?

Have you ever had a stranger ask you if you have a bird, and found yourself proudly answering yes, only to find that you're walking around in public with little dried squiggles of poop on the back of your shoulder? Unlike dogs, small birds such as parakeets aren't easy to potty train. It's easier to train yourself to change T-shirts more often!

There are two reasons your bird leaves presents on your T-shirts more often than you'd like. First, parakeets, like all parrots, poop often because they can fly. To fly, birds need to be streamlined and as light as possible, which is why some of their bones are hollow and also why they poop so often. A

bird who's holding in a load of poop is a heavier bird who has to work harder to fly. So nature has given birds a small place in their bodies to hold poop, forcing them to eliminate far more often than most other animals.

Secondly, parakeets, like many of the other smaller parrots, have a high metabolic rate. This means that they have to eat a lot to maintain their body weight and to keep everything working the way it should. So, if a parakeet eats often, she poops often. Now, how to get parakeet poop out of your new designer shirt . . .

Why Do Parakeets Like to Sit in High Places?

Prey animals, such as the parakeet, are vigilant creatures who like to have a good vantage point from which to spot lurking danger. Their lives depend on their keen eyesight and awareness, and where better to spot danger than from a high-up place?

Curtain rods, ceiling fans, and chandeliers make magnificent perching places for a parakeet, but they're not the safest places to perch. A ceiling fan is especially dangerous, and chandeliers may contain toxic metals. If you don't want to have to retrieve your beloved pet from high in the rafters, consider clipping his wings or offering him a safer place to fly.

BOW BEFORE ME,
THY INFERIOR BEINGS!

Some people theorize that allowing a bird to sit higher than your head makes him feel superior to you. This may be true for individual birds, but on the whole, a well-socialized parakeet should not be discouraged from sitting in a high spot sometimes. He feels safe up there! To make you both happier try hanging a playgym where your bird can watch the world to his little birdie heart's content.

Why Do Parakeets Chew on So Many Things?

All birds in the hookbill family, including your parakeet, are notorious chewers and view all wood, paper, and cloth as their domain to be chewed to bits when they so desire. Fortunately, the parakeet has one of the smaller beaks among the hookbills, so the damage is not as great as it might be with a larger parrot. But don't turn your back on a parakeet if you have expensive antiques or artwork—you might come home to find that your parakeet has made a few modifications to your priceless objects.

Parakeets in the wild have a lot to do. They have full-time jobs; they forage for food, search for water, build nests, and raise young. Your parakeet lives a much different life. She does not

WHAT?
MOBY DICK

need to expend nearly the amount of energy that her wild cousins do; yet she's still compelled to live as they live and has the same amount of energy. This is part of the reason it's so important that a parakeet be allowed to chew on safe items. Chewing also provides your parakeet with much-needed exercise and offers mental stimulation in an otherwise dull day—not many parakeet owners can be with their birds every moment. Provide your parakeet with plenty of chewable toys and perches, and don't become irritated with her when she chews them into toothpicks. At least she's not chewing your Picasso.

Toy Tips for Your Parakeet

You can't put a stop to destructive behavior, but you can try to direct your parakeet's energies to the proper items. Provide your bird with a wide variety of toys in a variety of materials:

- soft wood
- sisal rope
- mirrors
- leather
- lava rock
- hard plastic
- bells
- acrylic

Rotate different toys in and out of the cage on a weekly basis. This makes each toy seem new and interesting, and allows you to clean and disinfect the toys you've removed by using a 10 percent bleach solution and rinsing well in hot water. Remember to keep your parakeet's favorite toy inside the cage at all times—occasionally a toy can substitute for a friend or mate, and you won't want to take your parakeet's "buddy" away unless the behavior becomes problematic.

Why Do Parakeets Bite Sometimes (or All the Time!)?

Even the sweetest parakeets can become bitter biters. Biting is not a defense mechanism that birds generally use in the wild; it is a product of being held in captivity. When a bird is threatened or frightened, he uses his powers of flight to remove himself from the situation. A clipped or caged parakeet can't fly away, so he turns to other measures when he's afraid. Parakeets perceive situations differently than we do. Sticking your hand into a cage to retrieve your bird might seem fine to you, but it might be seen as an affront to your parakeet. Try to imagine the situation from your parakeet's perspective.

Once a bite is successful—the parakeet gets you to flee the

CHOMP!

scene after placing a nasty bite onto your finger—the behavior is instilled in him and he will repeat it. Here's one scenario: Your parakeet, for whatever reason, has bitten you. You react by screaming, jumping around, and running for a Band-Aid. The bird has just learned a valuable lesson: *If I bite, the threat goes away and I'm treated to a fabulous show of my owner screaming and jumping, which I love.* The next time you get bitten, do nothing. Just walk away and ignore your parakeet for a few minutes. Your bird can't imagine a worse fate than being ignored by a flock member. When the bird has calmed down, continue your contact with him.

Sometimes biting can be a sign of illness or injury. If you notice a drastic change in your parakeet, take him to your avian veterinarian.

Why Do Parakeets Seem Like the Perfect Snack for a Cat or a Dog?

Cats and dogs are programmed to hunt, and parakeets are prey animals who sit trapped in one spot all day, easy sport for Fido and Kitty. Would you go swimming with alligators? For a parakeet, living in a home with cats and dogs is like you taking the plunge with a bunch of hungry gators. Eventually, someone's going to get eaten, and it's not going to be the reptiles.

No matter how much training your dog and cat receive, you can never eliminate their instinct to kill small, fast-moving critters. It's important to remember that spaniels and retrievers are bred to hunt birds, terriers are bred to kill vermin and small animals, and sight hounds are bred to kill small, fast-moving

things. Isn't your parakeet a small, fast-moving object? Parakeet for lunch, anyone?

Cats are a primary killer of small birds, which doesn't make them bad animals, but does make them dangerous to your parakeet. Cats have a type of bacteria on their teeth and claws that are so deadly to birds, that one small scratch can kill a bird within twenty-four hours. If your dog or cat even so much as touches your parakeet, take the bird to the avian veterinarian right away. Kitty is cute and Fido is friendly but Polly the Parakeet is precious and doesn't want to become a midnight snack.

Nikki Moustaki has worked in aviculture and bird rescue and rehabilitation since 1988. She writes regularly about birds for *Bird Talk* magazine, *Birds USA*, and *Pet Product News*. Nikki also owns and hosts Birdy Works at www.birdyworks.com, a site dedicated to the care and training of companion birds. She is the author of several books about bird care and training, including *Why Do Cockatiels Do That?*

Buck Jones's humorous illustrations have appeared in numerous magazines (including *Dog Fancy* and *Cat Fancy*) and books. He is the illustrator for the best-selling books *Barking*, *Chewing*, *Digging*, *House-Training*, *Kittens! Why Do They Do What They Do?*, *Puppies! Why Do They Do What They Do?*, and *Why Do Cockatiels Do That?*

For more authoritative and fun facts about birds, including health-care advice, behavior tips, and insights into the special joys and overcoming the unique problems of bird ownership, go to your local pet shop, bookstore, or newsstand and pick up your copy of *Bird Talk* magazine today.

BowTie Press is a division of Fancy Publications, which is the world's largest publisher of pet magazines. For further information on your favorite pets, look for *Dog Fancy*, *Dogs USA*, *Cat Fancy*, *Cats USA*, *Horse Illustrated*, *Reptiles*, *Aquarium Fish*, *Rabbits*, *Ferrets USA*, and many more.